DATE DUE

To Boris – PG

Annick Press Ltd.

The publisher wishes to thank the Maintenance, Operations and Equipment
Engineering Office of the Ministry of Transportation for the Province of Ontario for
their assistance in the development of this book.

Canadian Cataloguing in Publication Data
Adams, Georgie
Highway builders

ISBN 1-55037-467-2 (bound) ISBN 1-55037-466-4 (pbk.)

1. Road machinery – Juvenile literature. I. Gregory,
Peter, 1947– . II. Title.

TE223.A33 1996   j629.225   C95-931365-6

Distributed in Canada by:
Firefly Books Ltd.
250 Sparks Avenue
Willowdale, ON   M2H 2S4

Published in the U.S.A. by Annick Press (U.S.) Ltd.
Distributed in the U.S.A. by:
Firefly Books (U.S.) Inc.
P.O. Box 1338, Ellicott Station
Buffalo, NY 14205

Printed and bound in China.

HIGHWAY BUILDERS

Georgie Adams   Peter Gregory

Annick Press Ltd.
Toronto • New York

READY TO START

Every day trucks and cars take people and the things they need from place to place on roads. But who built the roads and how did they do it?

First, large earth-moving machines, trucks and backhoes are needed to clear the land.

BACKHOE LOADERS

A backhoe is one of the most useful machines for clearing the site. It can dig all kinds of earth, clay and rubble and carry it away in its loader bucket. With just a flick of a switch in the cab, all four wheels can be turned so the backhoe can go forward or backward, or all four wheels can be turned to move the loader sideways, just like a crab!

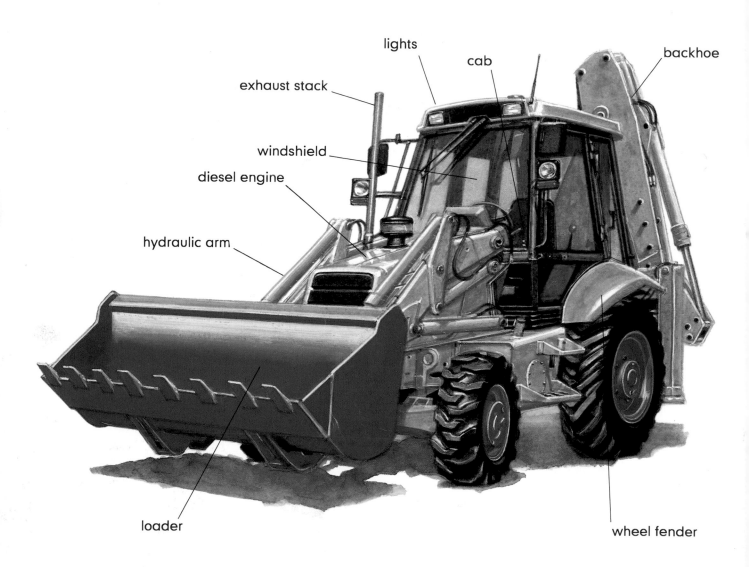

lights

cab

backhoe

exhaust stack

windshield

diesel engine

hydraulic arm

loader

wheel fender

This driver is using the hydraulic arms to lift the loader bucket, which is now full of earth. He can move it to dump the earth out or load it into a dump truck.

He can even use the shovel at the back to dig a ditch.

MOBILE CRANES

The mobile crane uses a telescopic boom to lift tonnes of building materials into the air, swing them around, and lower them to the ground. Why doesn't it tip over? It has special feet called outriggers that hold the crane firmly on the ground. It also has a heavy weight called a counterweight. These two things make sure that the crane will not fall over when it is working.

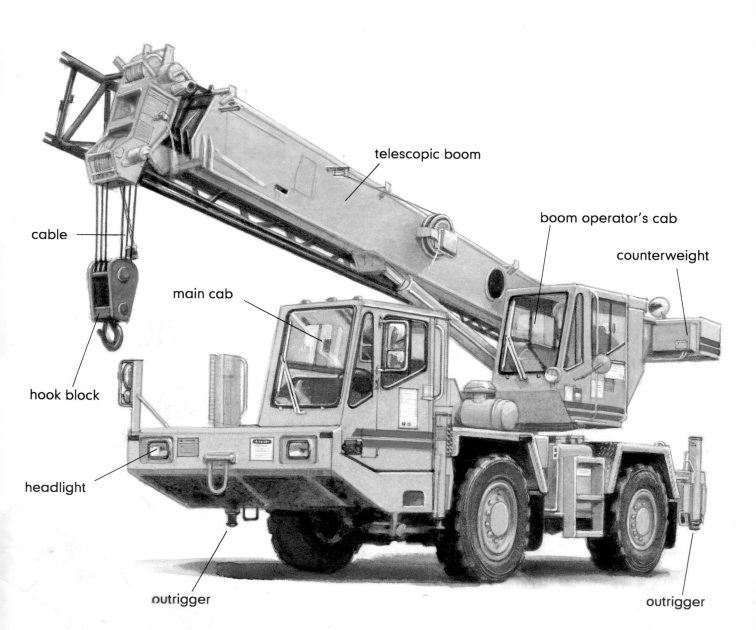

telescopic boom

boom operator's cab

counterweight

cable

main cab

hook block

headlight

outrigger

outrigger

Mobile cranes lift things like this drainage pipe with chains on a huge hook.

This crane is hoisting heavy steel girders to the top of the bridge. You can see the outriggers at the four corners, steadying the machine.

EXCAVATORS

The boom and bucket on the excavator are used for heavy digging. Like steel jaws, the bucket bites deep into the ground and scoops up huge loads of earth. Many other tools can be attached to do different jobs. Instead of tires, the excavator has steel tracks to move it over rugged land and up steep slopes without getting stuck.

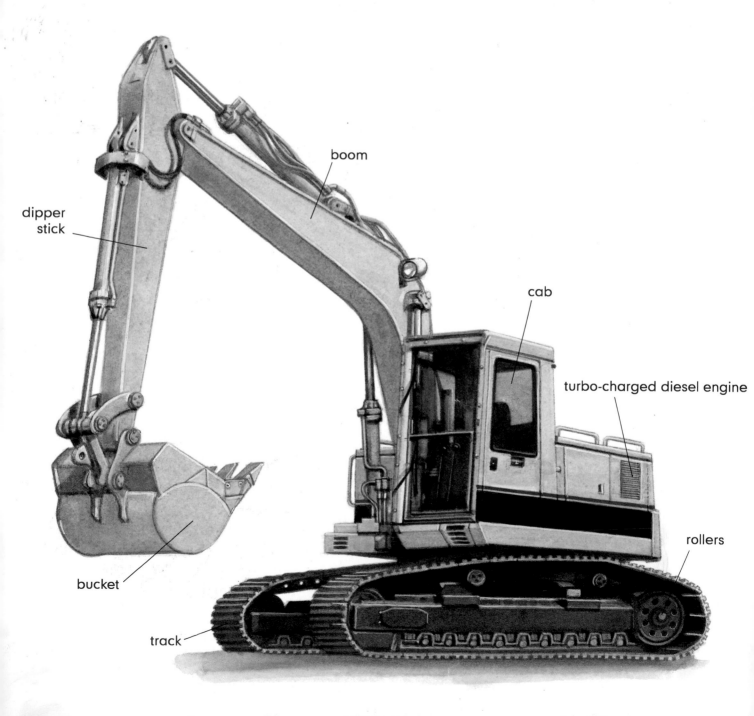

boom

dipper stick

cab

turbo-charged diesel engine

bucket

rollers

track

The hydraulic rock hammer breaks up rocks.

Another special bucket can dig out giant boulders.

Here, the grappling claw moves a load of tree trunks.

BULLDOZERS

Bulldozers push away mounds of earth and rocks with a large blade at the front.

They have steel tracks too. Each track looks like a belt. The tracks roll over a series of wheels with teeth on them. These teeth grab the track as it comes by and moves it along. The tracks grip the ground so that the bulldozer can crawl over all sorts of ground without sinking or getting stuck.

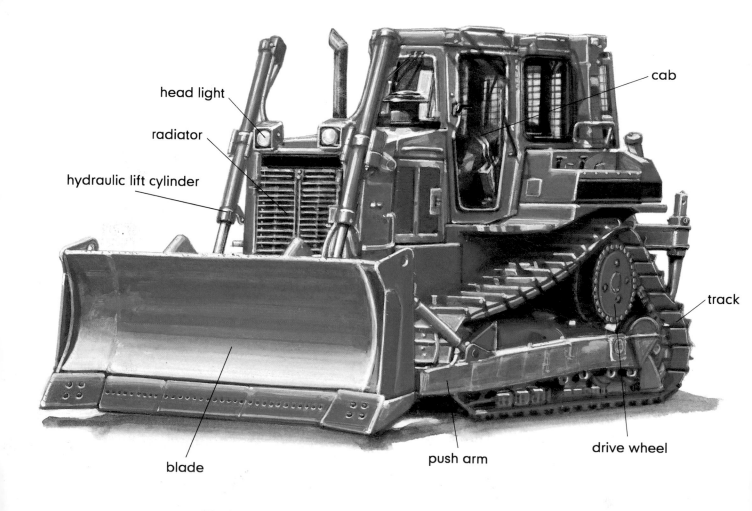

cab

head light

radiator

hydraulic lift cylinder

track

drive wheel

push arm

blade

The bulldozer uses two hydraulic arms to lift and tilt the front blade to move tonnes of dirt out of the way.

The bulldozer can also take out rocks and roots with the ripper tool attached to its back.

MAKING THE ROAD

The site is now clear. All the trees and rocks are gone. There are fences to show where the road will be, but there is still a lot of work to do! All those machines have left lumps and bumps and tracks all over. Now different machines will finish the road.

DUMP TRUCKS

Some of these trucks are giants. The tires are almost twice as tall as a person, and this truck can carry 136 tonnes at a time. That means it could carry about 27 elephants!

Dump trucks are also faster than the other earth-moving machines, so they are used to carry loads over long distances.

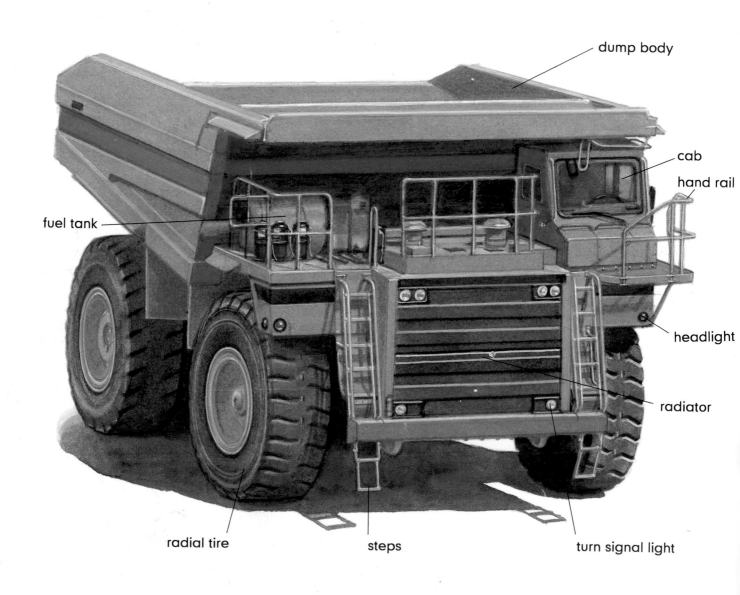

dump body

cab

hand rail

fuel tank

headlight

radiator

radial tire

steps

turn signal light

This dump truck is working with an excavator. The excavator loads dirt into the open back and the truck hauls it away.

These are articulated trucks. The cab and body of these trucks are jointed – they have a flexible construction that hooks together the cab and body – so that they can easily turn to unload.

MOTOR SCRAPERS

The road is not yet smooth enough; it still is full of lumps and bumps. Special machines scrape these away. The driver lowers the scraper bowl and the blade on the front of the bowl scrapes away the top layers of dirt.

The bowl has a sliding floor. It can be opened enough to allow earth to be scraped up inside the bowl. The earth piles up inside the bowl. After the dirt is scraped by the blade, it is shovelled onto a kind of escalator that carries it up into the bowl, away from the opening in the bottom.

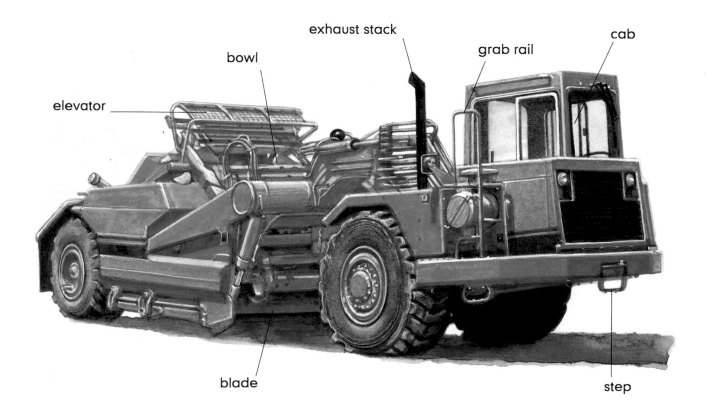

When the bowl is full, the floor slides shut, and the bowl is raised again. Then the scraper can drive away and dump the load.

Sometimes the scraper needs more power, and then a bulldozer might help push it.

COMPACTORS

The ground is smoother now, but it is still uneven. Now the big compactors start their job. Instead of tires, they have wheels that look like big drums. Each drum is covered with studded feet, arranged in a pattern.

With just one lever inside the cab, the driver can change the speed and direction of the compactor. It can then move forwards or backwards. Another lever raises or lowers the blade.

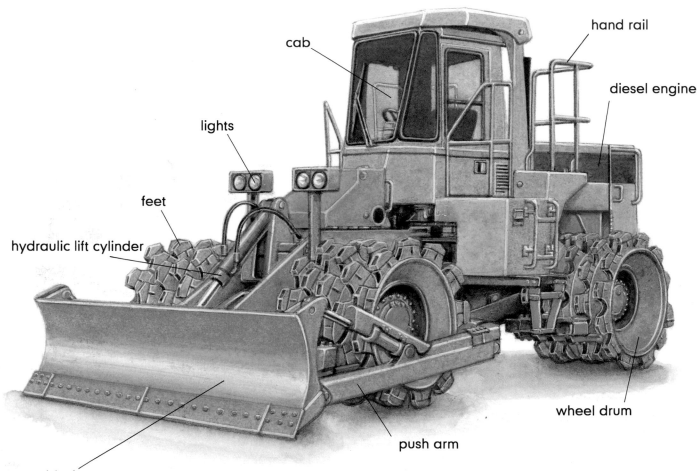

The blade spreads the earth and a powerful engine drives the compactor over the ground.

Each wheel drum has 65 steel feet, set in rows. As they roll over the bumps, the drums press the ground flat.

MOTOR GRADERS

Motor graders look like snow plows. They have steel blades that sweep layers of gravel or limestone over the road surface to level the road base. The blade can also be tilted upright to cut ditches or make banks along the side of the highway.

The wheels can lean to the right or left to add more pressure to the blade; the more pressure put on the blade, the deeper it will cut or scrape.

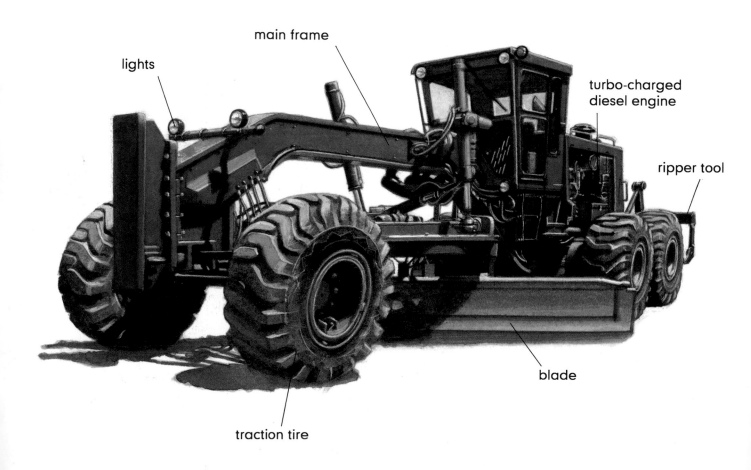

main frame

lights

turbo-charged diesel engine

ripper tool

blade

traction tire

The blade pushes the gravel out of the way just like a snow plow.

The road is not going to be level, but will slope down from the middle so that rain will run off the highway instead of making puddles all over it.

ROLLERS

Very heavy rollers like this one are always busy around the site, flattening out the road base. A roller is a type of compactor. It has two big drums made of steel. Each drum weighs as much as 6000 kilograms. (If you didn't have a roller, you would need about 25 bull moose or two white rhinos to do the job for you.)

This roller carries two large water tanks. When the roller is working over hot pavement, water is sprayed over the drums so that asphalt does not stick to them.

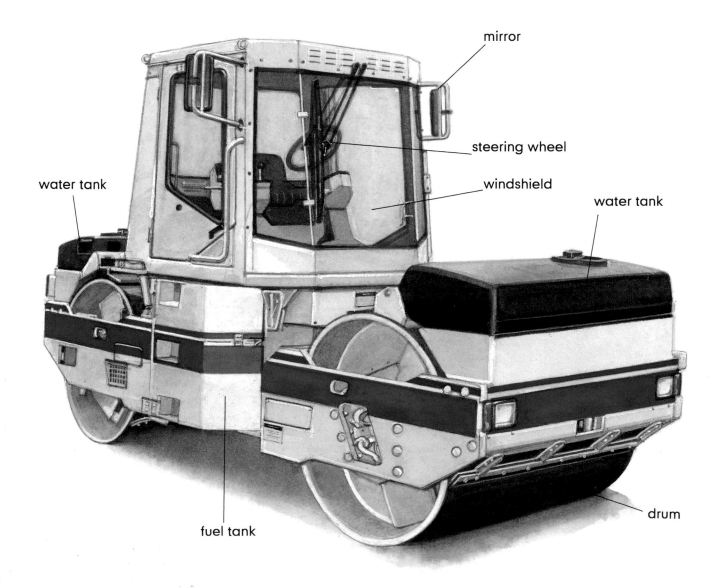

mirror

steering wheel

water tank

windshield

water tank

fuel tank

drum

The drums on this roller vibrate as they roll over rocks. The vibrating movement helps to crush the rocks.

This roller is working over hot asphalt, packing small chips into the pavement until it is smooth.

PAVERS AND CHIPPERS

Now that the surface is smooth and level, it is time to make the finished road.

First the paver lays a mat of asphalt pavement. This is a mixture of sand, gravel and liquid asphalt. Then a roller follows on behind, packing the hot asphalt until it is smooth.

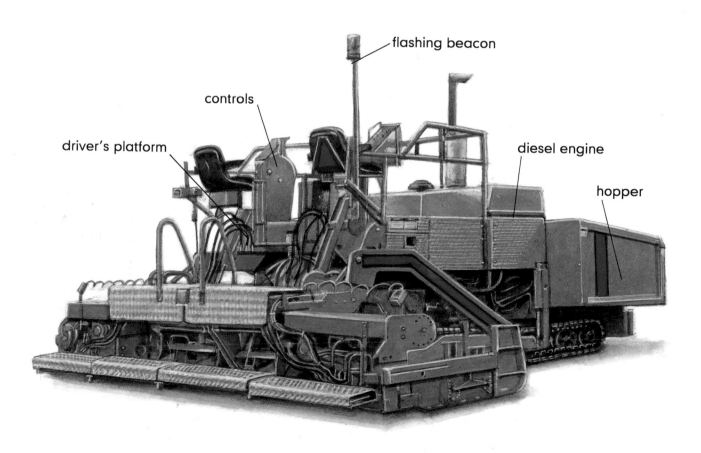

The asphalt is fed into the front of the paver by a truck. The paver heats the asphalt and spreads a layer on the road.

A chipper works nearby, paving a secondary road. It spreads stone chips on top of a layer of liquid asphalt. A compactor follows, rolling the road surface smooth.

FINISHING OFF

The new highway stretches away off in the distance. The work crews are putting up street lights and finishing the landscaping. The bulldozers, loaded on giant transport trucks, are the first passengers on the new highway. Soon traffic will be travelling down the new road and someone will be wondering, "How did they build this highway?"

Glossary

articulated

When a machine is "articulated", it means that two parts of it are connected by a joint or hinge. The cab and body of an articulated truck are linked or hinged together so that it can turn easily.

asphalt

This is a mixture of sand, gravel and liquid asphalt that is used to surface the road.

boom

This is a long lifting arm. Different tools can be attached to the boom "stick" to pick up and shovel heavy loads.

chips

Chips are small stones used for making the road surface.

elevator

This is a machine with paddles fixed to a belt which works like a moving staircase. The elevator on a motor scraper carries soil up and into the scraper bowl.

diesel engine

This type of engine has pistons which move up and down inside cylinders. As the pistons move up, they push air inside the cylinders into a very small space. The air gets hot. A pump squirts a special kind of oil into the hot air, making the oil burn. The burnt oil makes hot gases which force the pistons down again. The pistons are linked to the parts of the engine which turn the wheels and move the machine along.

hydraulic arm

The power to lift or push machinery is provided by an hydraulic arm. It has one large and one small cylinder, with a piston inside each.

It works like this: the cylinders are filled with a special kind of liquid and linked by a pipe. When one piston is rammed into the small cylinder, it pushes the liquid along the pipe into the large cylinder. It does this at great pressure. This forces the piston in the large cylinder to rise and produces the power to lift or push.

outriggers

These are extending metal legs that slide down from a steel case to hold a machine firmly on the ground while it is working.

ripper tool

This is a steel claw used for pulling out rocks and roots.

tracks

Tracks are steel belts which roll over cogged wheels and are driven by a motor. Tracks are used instead of wheels to move machines such as bulldozers over rugged and muddy ground without getting stuck.